365 REASONS

FOR SMILING

... in thoughts and pictures

WHITE STAR PUBLISHERS

365 REASONS

FOR SMILING

... in thoughts and pictures

CONTENTS

THOSE WHO CAN LAUGH ARE MASTERS OF THE WORLD

LIST OF CONTRIBUTORS - PHOTO CREDITS

TRAINING

Is it really so important to smile? It really seems so. Many people have thought so ever since ancient times. It is also good for the muscles, the heart and the spirit. Researchers at the best universities say so: laughter increases the production of endorphin, fundamental for bodily well-being, useful for alleviating stress, reducing anxiety and pain and improving circulation. It is also a stimulus for the facial and diaphragmatic muscles, reinforces immunity defenses and makes us more attractive, more beautiful. It's a good way, easy and light, economical and carefree, to increase self-esteem and confidence in oneself. I laugh, therefore I exist, to paraphrase a famous saying.

Laughter arouses positive emotions and this sometimes is a very effective therapeutic instrument to stay healthy or get better: those who are able to maintain a good level of happiness improve the quality of their lives.

It was a sign of wisdom for the Ancients, of intelligence for contemporaries: those who know how to laugh and laugh at themselves are a step ahead of others, since they can perceive hidden aspects of reality. It's like putting on a pair of colored glasses: the world, though it stays the same in form, changes in substance, through a continuously moving kaleidoscope.

There are many ways of laughing. It can simply be a physical reaction to being tickled or frightened, embarrassed or excited. One can smile tenderly when looking at a child, or receiving a meaningful glance. We half smile at a proverb, we laugh with our mouth wide open at an amusing joke. We show our teeth at a wisecrack, we explode in uncontrollable laughter at the comedian. A sarcastic

TO SMILE

remark, when irony is dressed in cynicism, often makes us laugh all the same, even with a touch of bitterness. And a sardonic and stinging laugh on the face of your interlocutor is a way to say, "Let's not take ourselves too seriously, let's joke about our weaknesses and obsessions, let's not be ashamed of what we are."

For example, we can only roll about laughing when we see the dog Muttley in the cartoons, who sniggers at every misfortune of his master, the hapless Dick Dastardly. Or we can only be transfixed and thoughtful when we see the most famous smile, the enigmatic smile of the Mona Lisa, immortalized in Leonardo's picture in the Louvre. Because, in any case, the smile is captivating, intriguing: also in advertisements for watches the hands are intentionally set to ten past ten, precisely to simulate the splendid expression of the human face.

There is more subtle difference between laughter and smile, comedy and irony, according to the thickness of the layer separating reality and truth. What is comic is the clown's red nose, Charlie Chaplin's bowler hat and stick, the monkey scratching its head, the comical or ridiculous effect of how human beings can become the object of derision, but in a good sense, and without identification. Henri Bergson said that a comic situation is "a momentary anaesthesia of the heart" because it completely removes the identification with the person who is the subject of the laughter. Ironically, Charlie Chaplin as a dictator plays with the world in the form of a ball: it is a more bitter smile that also involves the head, and which requires a greater rational involvement and identification with the person who is made fun of. It is no accident that the best actor is the one who makes the audience not only laugh but cry, who easily and naturally moves his audience from the most carefree laughter to being intensely moved.

We laugh about everything human, vices and virtues, habits and desires, the worst intentions and the greatest successes. About what we love and at the same time hate, about what we understand and what will always remain a mystery. About love, about women and men, about relationships between women and men, about children, about animals. We take off conventions and seriousness to put on a lighter and more comfortable suit which is made of spontaneousness and complicity. A wink in exchange for a sulk. A smile instead of a tear. It is no accident that today, in our way of communicating, we embellish smiling messages or e-mails with little faces, also in a work context: we only need a colon, a hyphen and a bracket ... :-)

Laughing is a question of timing. The timing of comedy in the theater also survive in real life: the expectation, the creation of suspense and the punch line, which explodes in an unexpected, sparkling reaction. It's all in the timing: if the wait is too long, if the punch line comes early ... there is no more joke and the moment is wasted, for ever.

Can we learn to smile? It often happens in the group that there is someone who did not understand the joke or needs to have it explained, thus losing the comic effect of the moment. But good training can do miracles. Be careful to exercise daily, to moderate tone and put things right. Let's try, even if perhaps *not everyone is able to do it. Let's repeat it ceaselessly, with a smile on our lips. We can begin, for example, to laugh at ourselves, with a greater degree of knowledge of self. It is useful for not taking ourselves seriously, the minimum necessary to face life events with the right detachment. Or we can begin by reading this book, a little manual to learn how to smile, perhaps to keep on the bedside table or the breakfast table: why not a coffee sweetened with a smile? Training, with a short phase daily in front of an unusual or curious image, to move all the muscles of the face together, as many as 36 according to anatomy manuals, and facing what life has in store for us with the right dose of happiness.*

The sentences embrace proverbs and poetic verses, ironic wisecracks that sometimes approach sarcasm, amusing obervations and jokes by masters. A quiver full of arrows capable of putting the darkest days right. And the archers are diverse authors, very different from each other: from humourists par excellence, like Oscar Wilde, Groucho Marx and Woody Allen, to American television personalities, Italian comedians, British authors and Russian writers. The images are accompanied, here and there, by poetic sentences dedicated to the magic of a smile written by authoritative authors of every epoch. In short, with the right glasses, the world will not be the same as before.

Chiara Schiavano and Carlo Batà

1

January

I'm so excited about the new year.
Unfortunately, I have no good resolutions
to make because I'm already perfect.

– Anonymous

JANUARY

2

January

If at first you don't succeed,
skydiving is not for you.

– Bill Murray

3

January

All animals, except man, know that
the principal business of life is to enjoy it.

– Samuel Butler

4

January

People change and forget
to tell each other.

– Lillian Florence Hellman

5

January

Everyone wants to save the world, but few help Mum to wash the dishes.

– Roland Topor

6

January

Don't take life too seriously,
you'll never get out of it alive.

– Elbert Hubbard

7

January

When Armageddon takes place,
parking is going to be
a major problem.

– James G. Ballard

January

The trouble with our times is that
the future is not what it used to be.

– Paul Valéry

9

January

"Oh, you're taking a course in conversation?." "Yes."

– Steve Martin

10

January

Policemen appear so sincere, without telling you anything.

– Agatha Christie

11

January

Your wrinkles either show that you're nasty, cranky,
and senile, or that you're always smiling.

– Carlos Santana

12

January

Laziness is nothing more than
the habit of resting before you get tired.

– Jules Renard

13
January

Cats are intended to teach us that
not everything in nature has a purpose.

– Garrison Keillor

14
January

Cats can work out mathematically
the exact place to sit that
will cause most inconvenience.

– Pam Brown

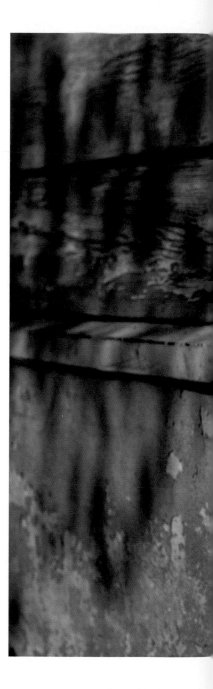

15

January

We haven't got a plan
so nothing can go wrong!

– *Spike Milligan*

16

January

In real life, I assure you, there is no
such thing as algebra.

– *Fran Lebowitz*

17
January

Little things seem nothing,
but they give peace.

– Georges Bernanos

18
January

The most affectionate creature
in the world is a wet dog.

– Ambrose Bierce

19

January

Monkeys are superior to men in this: when
a monkey looks into a mirror, he sees a monkey.

– *Malcolm de Chazal*

20

January

Inappropriate behavior makes me laugh.

– Will Ferrell

21

January

If you want the world to beat a path to your door,
just try to take a nap on a Saturday afternoon.

– Sam Ewing

22

January

You can't stay mad at someone
who makes you laugh.

– Jay Leno

23

January

If love is the answer, could you please
rephrase the question?

– *Lily Tomlin*

24

January

A smile is the light in the window
of your face that tells people
you're at home.

– Anonymous

25

January

You can learn many things from children.
How much patience you have,
for instance.

– Franklin P. Jones

26

January

It is more comfortable to feel that we are a slight improvement
on a monkey than such a fallin' off from the angels.

– Finley Peter Dunne

27

January

Call it a clan, call it a network, call it a tribe, call it a family.
Whatever you call it, whoever you are, you need one.

– Jane Howard

28

January

I love good creditable acquaintance.
I love to be the worst of the company.

– Jonathan Swift

29

January

People who never laugh are not serious people.

– Fryderyk Chopin

30

January

I have no special talent. I am only passionately curious.

– Albert Einstein

31

January

Properly trained,
a man can be dog's best friend.

– Corey Ford

1

February

Keys are awkward and can get lost.
It's better to have someone who can open
the door, if possible with a smile.

– Dino Basili

FEBRUARY

2

February

An appeaser is one who feeds a crocodile,
hoping it will eat him last.

– Winston Churchill

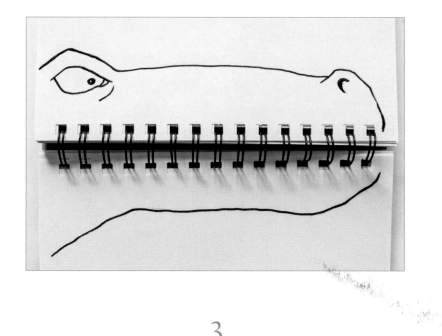

3

February

Dinosaurs didn't read.
Now they are extinct!

– Anonymous

4

February

The goose is the animal considered a symbol of stupidity, because of the nonsense that men have written with his feathers.

– Anonymous

5

February

Roads are no place for naive chickens dreaming of nirvana.

– Shalom Auslander

6

February

Gorgeous hair is the best revenge.

– Ivana Trump

7

February

The comic is the tragic
seen from behind.

– Gérard Genette

8

February

Every child is an artist.
The problem is how to remain
an artist once we grow up.

– Pablo Picasso

9

February

One possesses an immense fortune
when one is able to rejoice.

– George Bernard Shaw

10

February

You know you're getting old when
the candles cost more than the cake.

– Bob Hope

11

February

I've never met a problem that
a proper cupcake couldn't fix.

– Sarah Ockler

12
February

Growing up is losing some illusions,
in order to acquire others.

– *Virginia Woolf*

13
February

An optimist is a man who orders
dozens of oysters, planning
to pay for them with
the pearl he might find.

– *Theodor Fontane*

14

February

A dreamer is someone
whose feet are firmly
grounded in clouds.

– Ennio Flaiano

15

Man is derived from the monkey.
And the monkey is rather annoyed about it.

– Paolo Dune

16

February
It wasn't love at first sight.
It took a full five minutes.

– Lucille Ball

17

February

All you need is love. But a little
chocolate now and then doesn't hurt.

– Charles M. Schulz

18

February

When his daughter marries, the father loses the dowry,
but regains the bathroom and the telephone.

– Robert Lembke

19

February

A ruffled mind
makes a restless pillow.

– Charlotte Brontë

20

February

Purring is like smile aloud.

– Hank Ketcham

21

February

If life is becoming a race,
could it be time to slow down?

– Evinda Lepins

22

February

One should always play fair...
when one has the winning cards.

– Oscar Wilde

23

February

A good yard may have some weeds.

– Thomas Fuller

24

February

Gardening is not a rational act.

– Margaret Atwood

25

February

It's not the load that breaks you down,
it's the way you carry it.

– Lou Holtz

26

February

In the history of the world,
no one has ever washed a rented car.

– Lawrence Summers

27

February

Vehicular Darwinism based on survival of the quickest.

– Raymond L. Atkins

February

You know, somebody actually complimented me
on my driving today. They left a little note on the windscreen,
it said "Parking Fine."

– Tommy Cooper

1

March

I have had a perfectly wonderful evening,
but this wasn't it.

– Groucho Marx

MARCH

2
March

A banker is a fellow who lends you
his umbrella when the sun is shining, but
wants it back the minute it begins to rain.

– Mark Twain

3
March

Everything is funny as long
as it is happening to somebody else.

– Will Rogers

4

March

The grass may be greener
on the other side of the fence
but you still have to mow it.

– Proverb

5

March

The difference between stupidity and genius
is that genius has its limits.

– Albert Einstein

6

March

From the sublime to the ridiculous
there is but one step.

– Napoleon Bonaparte

7

March

Cleaning your house while your kids
are still growing up is like shoveling
the walk before it stops snowing.

– Phyllis Diller

8

March

Architecture is the art
of how to waste space.

– Philip Johnson

9

March

Believe only half of what you see
and nothing that you hear.

– Edgar Allan Poe

10
March
I wondered if it was blasphemous
to tell God that rainbows are kitsch.

– *Steve Toltz*

11

March

The best way to show
a giraffe your affection,
is to knit a scarf for it.

– Anonymous

12

March

The shortest distance
between two people is a smile.

– Victor Borge

13

March

Never measure the height of a mountain
until you have reached the top.
Then you will see how low it was.

– *Dag Hammarskjöld*

14

March

Anything good in life
is either illegal, immoral or fattening.

– *George Bernard Shaw*

15

March

People who keep stiff upper lips
find that it's damn hard to smile.

– *Judith Guest*

16

March

Barbershop conversations
are irrefutable proof that
heads exist for the sake of hair.

– Karl Kraus

17
March

Some years ago I got my head together.
I'm not the nutter of before:
now I'm the nutter of the future.

– Gianni Monduzzi

18
March

My theory of evolution
is that Darwin was adopted.

– Steven Wrights

19
March

If you can laugh about something,
you can also change it.

– Richard Bandler

20
March

If you can't convince them,
confuse them.

– Confucius

21

March

A well-developed sense of humor
is the pole that adds balance to your steps
as you walk the tightrope of life.

– William Arthur Ward

22

March

If we could truly see ourselves the way others see us
we'd disappear on the spot.

– Emil Cioran

23
March

Have no fear of perfection,
you'll never reach it.

– Salvador Dalí

24
March

I am fond of pigs.
Dogs look up to us.
Cats look down on us.
Pigs treat us as equals.

– Winston Churchill

25
March

The golden rule of work is that
the boss's jokes are always funny.

– Robert Paul

26
March

Humor is the most important
defense mechanism.

– Sigmund Freud

27
March

No one can change their face,
but some people go too far.

– Totò

28
March

Astronomy's much more fun
when you're not an astronomer.

– Brian May

29
March

You can't depend on your eyes
when your imagination
is out of focus.

– Mark Twain

30
March

Before you put on a frown,
make absolutely sure
there are no smiles available.

– Jim Begg

31
March

Most dogs don't think they're human;
they know they are.

– Jane Swan

1

April

You grow up the day
you have the first real laugh at yourself.

– Ethel Barrymore

APRIL

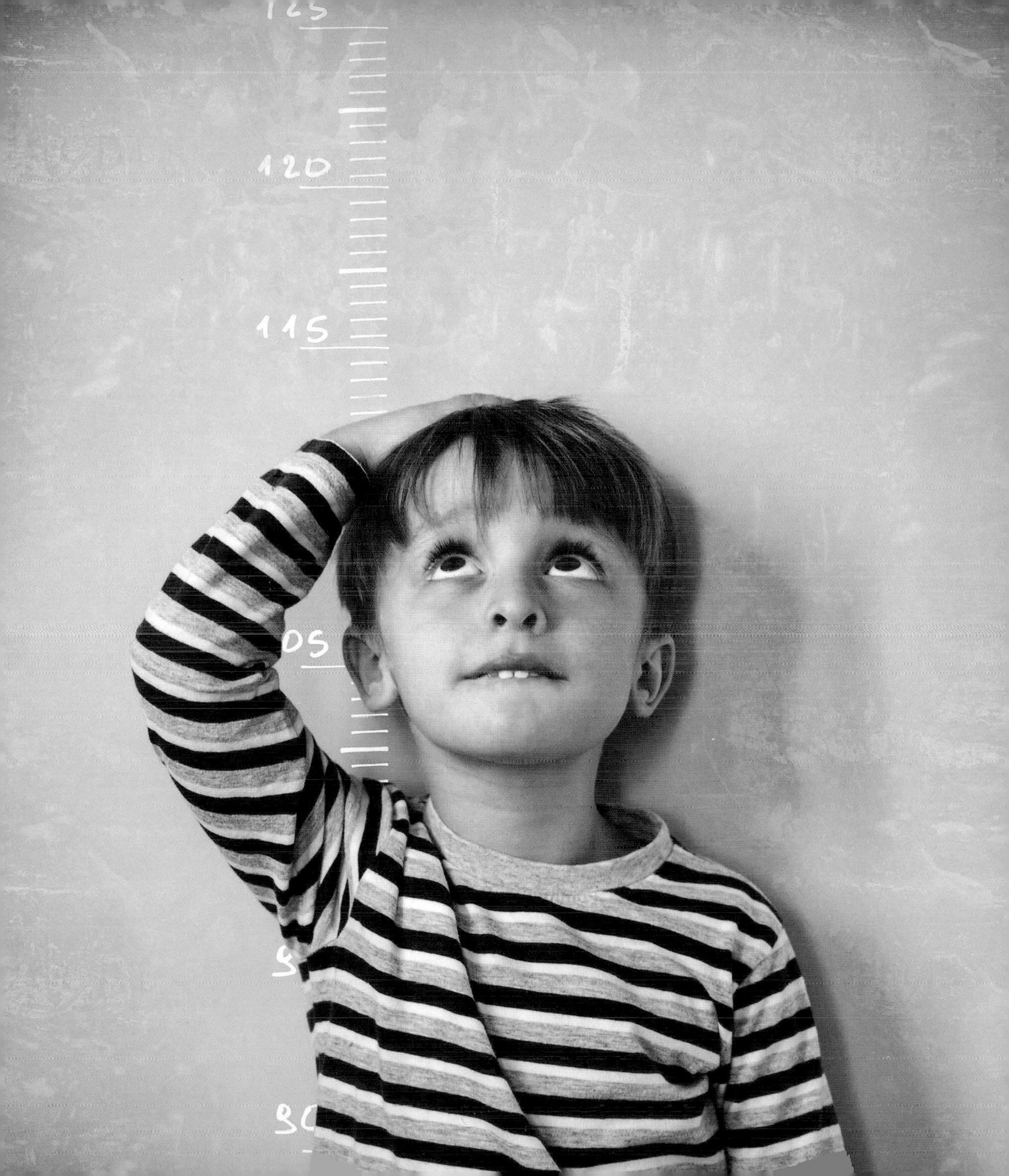
120
115

2

April

Eating is one of the four goals of life...
what the other three are,
no one has ever known.

– Chinese proverb

3

April

The second day of a diet
is always easier than the first.
By the second day you're off it.

– Jackie Gleason

4
April

One's company,
two's a crowd,
and three's a party.

– Andy Warhol

5
April

Sometimes being a brother
is even better than being a superhero.

– Marc Brown

6

April

You're never fully dressed without a smile.

– Martin Charnin

7

April

He who laughs last, probably didn't get the joke.

– Arthur Bloch

8

April

Most people deserve each other.

– Arthur Bloch

9

April

To feel at home, stay at home.

– Clifton Fadiman

10
April

A clown is like aspirin,
only he works twice as fast.

– Groucho Marx

11
April

Life is what happens
while you charging your phone.

– Anonymous

12

April

I'd rather be an optimist and a fool
than a pessimist and right.

– Albert Einstein

13

April

Fortune loves people
who are not too sensible.

– Erasmus of Rotterdam

14

April

It's not the size of the dog in the fight,
it's the size of the fight in the dog.

– Mark Twain

15

April

No man in the world has more courage than
the man who can stop after eating one peanut.

– Channing Pollock

16

April

The thing I fear most is fear.

– Michel de Montaigne

17
April

If a man smiles all the time,
he's probably selling
something that doesn't work.

– George Carlin

18
April

If God wanted us to fly,
He would have given us tickets.

– Mel Brooks

19
April

Cats find humans useful domestic animals.

– Georges Mikes

20
April

The caterpillar does all the work,
but the butterfly gets all the publicity.

– George Carlin

21

April

Dogs have owners,
cats have staff.

– Anonymous

22

April

We need to accept the fact that
for a few days we are monkeys
and for a few days statues.

– Boris Makaresko

23

April

If monkeys had the talent of parrots,
they could be ministers.

– Nicolas de Chamfort

24

April

A good neighbor is a fellow who smiles at you
over the back fence, but doesn't climb over it.

– Arthur Baer

25

April

A neurotic is a man who builds a castle in the air. A psychotic is the
man who lives in it. A psychiatrist is the man who collects the rent.

– Jerome Lawrence

26
April

We make our friends; we make our enemies;
but God makes our next-door neighbor.

– Gilbert Keith Chesterton

27
April

Always remember that you are absolutely unique.
Just like everyone else.

– Margaret Mead

28
April

Admiration: our polite recognition
of another's resemblance to ourselves.

– Ambrose Bierce

29
April

The surest sign that intelligent life
exists elsewhere in the universe
is that it has never tried to contact us.

– Bill Watterson

30
April

Getting to the top is optional.
Getting down is mandatory.

– Ed Viesturs

1

May

Philosophy is that thing whose only use is in comforting us of its uselessness.

– Jean Louis Auguste Commerson

MAY

2

May

The imaginary friends I had as a kid
dropped me because their friends
thought I didn't exist.

– Aaron Machado

3

May

In times like these,
talking of nothing
is at least something

– Pierre Dac

4

May

I have never developed indigestion
from eating my words.

– Winston Churchill

5

May

Do not put off until tomorrow what you can do after tomorrow.

– Alphonse Allais

6

May

Insanity: doing the same thing
over and over again and
expecting different results.

– Albert Einstein

7

May

Man is most nearly himself
when he achieves the seriosness
of a child at play.

– Heraclites

8

May

If you pretend to be good,
the world takes you very seriously.

– Oscar Wilde

9

May

Laughter is the jump from the
possible into the impossible.

– Georges Bataille

10

May

A century ago, people laughed at the notion that we were descended from monkeys. Today, the individuals most offended by that claim are the monkeys.

– Jacob M. Appel

11

May

Like in the zoo, you will always find lots of monkeys but very few lions.

– Nabil N. Jamal

12

May

If you have always done it that way,
it is probably wrong.

– Charles Franklin Kettering

13

May

A smile makes the road
twice a growl.

– Robert Baden-Powell

14

May

I never forget a face,
but in your case I'll be glad
to make an exception.

– Groucho Marx

15

May

Everyone seems to have
a clear idea of how other
people should lead their
lives, but none about
his or her own.

– Paulo Coelho

16

May

When the winds of change blow,
some people build walls and others build windmills.

– Chinese proverb

17

May

Sometimes I'd like to get inside your head
to have the sensation of a complete vacuum.

– Groucho Marx

18
May

Marriage is the bond between a person
who never remembers anniversaries
and another who never forgets them.

– Ogden Nash

19
May

The war between the sexes is the only one
in which both sides sleep with the enemy.

– Quentin Crisp

20

May

The secret of a happy marriage remains a secret.

– *Henny Youngman*

21
May

A great pleasure in life is doing
what people say you cannot do.

– Walter Bagehot

22
May

I hope that while so many people
are out smelling the flowers,
someone is taking the time to plant some.

– Herbert Rappaport

23

May

A man with his head in a hot oven
and his feet in a freezer has statistically
an average body temperature.

– Charles Bukowski

24

May

Do not do unto others as you expect
they should do unto you.
Their tastes may not be the same.

– George Bernard Shaw

25

May

Never argue with an idiot,
people may not be able to tell the difference.

– Arthur Bloch

26

May

There are no rules of architecture
for a castle in the clouds.

– Gilbert Keith Chesterton

27

May

Conversation about the weather
is the last refuge of the unimaginative.

– Oscar Wilde

28
May

If you help a friend in need,
he is sure to remember you
the next time he's in need.

– Arthur Bloch

29
May

Whoever said
you can't buy happiness
forgot little puppies.

– Gene Hill

30

May

Every man at the bottom of his heart
believes that he is a born detective.

– John Buchan

31

May

Humorists always sit at the children's table.

– Woody Allen

1

June

A woman should be like a single flower,
not a whole bouquet.

– *Anna Held*

JUNE

2

June

Insanity is hereditary; you get it from your children.

– Sam Levenson

3

June

Anyone who says sunshine brings happiness has never danced in the rain.

– Anonymous

4

June

It's a bit of a headache being a perfectionist.
You're never satisfied.

– Cherie Lunghi

5

June

The secret to modeling is not being perfect.
What one needs is a face that people can identify in a second.

– Karl Lagerfeld

6

June

I understood that I had got old
when all the guests at my birthday
gathered around the cake
to warm their hands.

– *George Burns*

7

June

You are what you eat.
What would you like to be?

– *Julie Murphy*

8

June

A smile is like a toothbrush.
You have to use it often to keep your teeth clean.

– Japanese proverb

9

June

The lion does not need the whole world to fear him,
only those nearest where he roams.

– A. J. Darkholme

10

June

The first condition of understanding
a foreign country is to smell it.

– Rudyard Kipling

11

June

If men had not existed,
dogs would have invented them.

– Clifford D. Simak

12

June

Problems become unfit
when you place them under your feet.

– Constance Chuks Friday

13

June

Youth ends when
your favourite football player
is younger than you.

– David Trueba

14
June

I must confess,
I was born at a very early age.

– Groucho Marx

15
June

The best contribution
each community can make
is giving milk to children.

– Winston Churchill

16

June

I believe the world to be a muffin pan,
and there certainly are a lot of muffins here.

– Aaron Funk

17

June

Days should begin with an embrace, a kiss, a caress and a coffee.
Because breakfast must be big.

– Charles M. Schulz

18

June

Success is a little like wrestling a gorilla.
You don't quit when you're tired.
You quit when the gorilla is tired.

– Robert Strauss

19

June

One can know a man from his laugh.

– Fyodor Dostoyevsky

20
June

Rivalry doesn't help anybody.

– Peter Jackson

21
June

Jealousy is a dog's bark
which attracts thieves.

– Karl Kraus

22

June

Don't accept your dog's admiration
as conclusive evidence that you are wonderful.

– Ann Landers

23

June

I have to exercise in the morning
before my brain figures out what I'm doing.

– *Anonymous*

24

June

Kilometers are shorter than miles.
Save gas, take your next trip in kilometers.

– George Carlin

25

June

The bicycle is a curious vehicle.
Its passenger is its engine.

– John Howard

26

June

I just got back from a pleasure trip.
I drove my mother-in-law to the airport.

−Milton Berle

27

June

An idealist is one who,
on noticing that roses smell better
than a cabbage, concludes that
they will also make better soup.

– Henry L. Mencken

28

June

A day without a laugh
is a wasted day.

– Charlie Chaplin

29
June

It is inconceivable how much wit
it requires to avoid being ridiculous.

– Nicolas de Chamfort

30
June

The only exercise I excel at
is jumping to conclusions.

– James Nathan Miller

1

July

It is easy to be beautiful;
it is difficult to appear so.

– *Frank O'Hara*

JULY

2
July

Patience is something you admire
in the driver behind you,
but not in the one ahead.

– Bill McGlashen

3
July

If you think nobody cares
if you're alive, try missing
a couple of car payments.

– Earl Wilson

4

July

One laughs unpleasantly at others
above all when one cannot laugh at oneself.

– Paul Léautaud

5

July

A woman is frank
when she does not lie uselessly.

– Anatole France

6
July

The problem with people who say
monsters don't really exist is that they're
almost never saying it to the monsters.

– Seanan McGuire

7
July

When I was young I thought
that money was the most important
thing in life; now that I am old
I know that it is.

– Oscar Wilde

8

July

When an elephant is in trouble,
even a frog will kick him.

– Indian proverb

9

July

Expecting the world to treat you fairly
because you are a good person
is a little like expecting the bull not to
attack you because you are a vegetarian.

– Dennis Wholey

10

July

If you carry your childhood with you,
you never become older.

– Tom Stoppard

11

July

When a child is locked in the bathroom
with water running and he says
he's doing nothing but the dog
is barking, call the emergency number.

– Erma Bombeck

12
July

There are people who talk,
talk and only talk... Until finally,
they find something to say.

– *Sacha Guitry*

13
July

It is madness for sheep
to talk peace with a wolf.

– *Friedrich Nietzsche*

14

July

You can only chase a butterfly for so long.

– Jane Yolen

15

July

In love, the one who flees wins only if someone follows.

– Roberto Gervaso

16

July

Those who don't jump will never fly.

– Leena Ahmad Almashat

17
July

If evolution really works,
how come mothers
only have two hands?

– Milton Berle

18
July

Siblings: children of the same
parents, each of whom is perfectly
normal until they get together.

– Sam Levenson

19

July

When you're eight-years-old
nothing is your business.

– Lenny Bruce

20

July

People don't notice whether it's winter
or summer when they're happy.

– Anton Chekhov

21
July

Fishes live in the sea, as men do a-land:
the great ones eat up the little ones.

– William Shakespeare

22
July

Grab shell, dude!

– Crush (Finding Nemo)

23
July

I named my dog Stay,
so I can say:
"Come here, Stay!
Come here, Stay!"

– *Steven Wright*

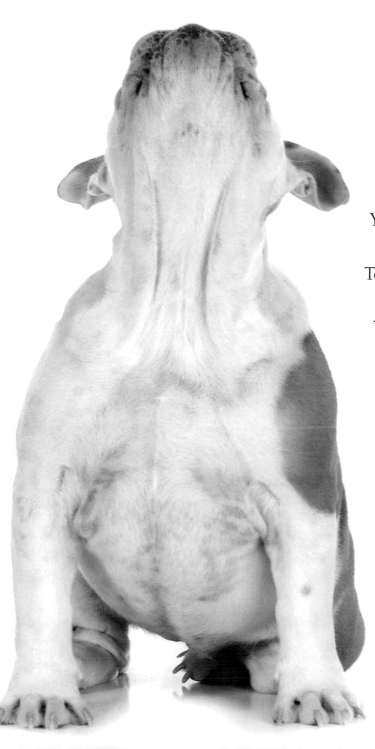

24
July

Yesterday I was a dog.
Today I'm a dog.
Tomorrow I'll probably
still be a dog. Sigh!
There's so little hope
for advancement.

– Charles M. Schulz

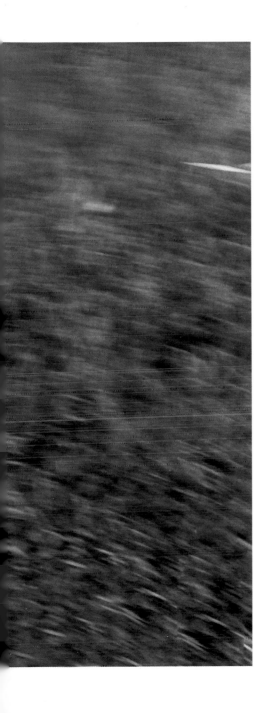

25
July

It is much easier to become
a father than to be one.

Kent Nerburn

26
July

Two things can save us in life:
to love and laugh.
If you have one of them it is fine.
If you have both you are invincible.

– Tarun Tejpal

27

July

What is a home without children? Quiet.

– Henny Youngman

28
July

Certain people believe that genius is hereditary. Others don't have children!

– Marcel Achard

29

July

As a child I was the type of child
with whom my mother told me
never to play.

– Leopold Fechtner

30
July

The main purpose of children's parties is to remind you that there are children worse than your own.

– Katharine Whitehorn

31
July

All generalizations are dangerous, even this one.

– Alexandre Dumas fils

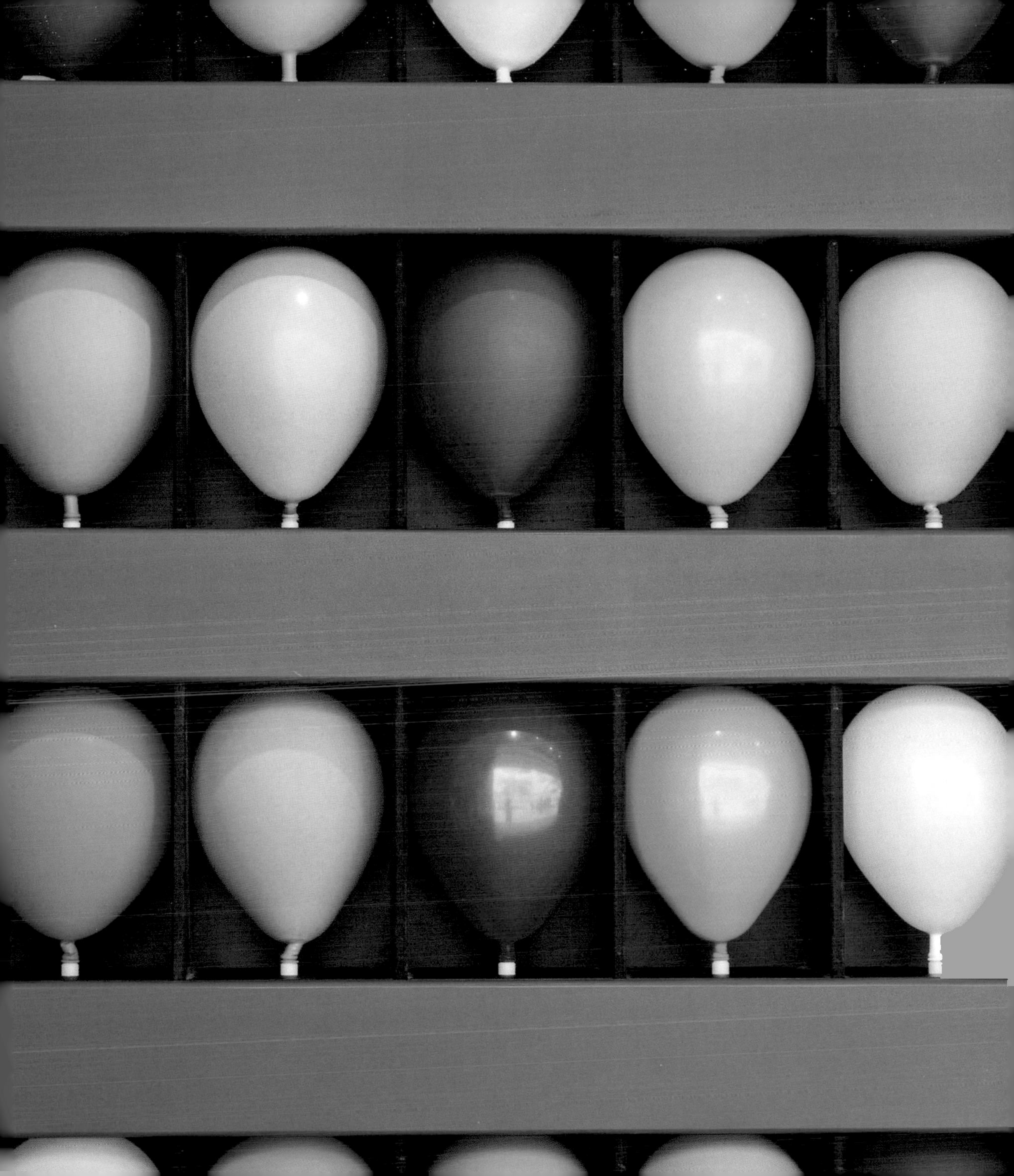

1

August

A two-year-old is like having a blender,
but you don't have a top for it.

– Jerry Seinfeld

AUGUST

2
August

Having one child makes you a parent;
having two you are a referee.

– *David Frost*

3
August

It's never too late to have a happy childhood.

– *Tom Robbins*

4

In philosophy if you aren't moving
at a snail's pace you aren't moving at all.

– Iris Murdoch

5

August

I am always doing what I cannot do yet,
in order to learn how to do it.

– Vincent van Gogh

6

August

You pretend to believe that the earth goes around the sun;
but deep down you're convinced it goes around you.

– Miguel Zamacoïs

7

August

Friends are relatives you make for yourself.

– Eustache Deschamps

No man needs a vacation so much as the man who has just had one.

– *Elbert Hubbard*

9

August

As we get older, we lose many of our defects:
we don't need them any more.

– Paul Claudel

10

August

Americans will put up with anything
provided it doesn't block traffic.

– Dan Rather

11

August

Isn't it amazing
how much stuff we get done
the day before vacation?

– Zig Ziglar

12

August

Man is 80% water. Before you measure
yourself you need to find out about
the tide times.

– Pierre Légaré

13

August

When a new baby laughs
for the first time a new fairy is born,
and as there are always new babies
there are always new fairies.

– James Matthew Barrie

14

August

Two watermelons cannot be held
under one arm.

– Turkish proverb

15

August

If you don't have a smile, I'll give you one of mine.

– Anonymous

16

August

Perfect communication exists.
It is a row.

– Stefano Benni

17

August

It's easy to be friends with
when shares the same opinions.

– Alexandre Dumas

18

August

I don't know why I had to fall in love with someone
who's more stubborn than I am.

– Cassandra Clare

19

August

The problem with people who have no vices is that generally you can
be pretty sure they're going to have some pretty annoying virtues.

– Elizabeth Taylor

20

August

The secret of living a long time is:
eat half, walking twice, three times to laugh
and to love without measure.

– Chinese proverb

21
August

My sister has the best sister in the world.

– *Anonymous*

22
August

I believe that happy girls are the prettiest girls.

– *Audrey Hepburn*

23
August

Grown-ups never understand anything
by themselves, and it is exhausting
for children to have to provide
explanations over and over again.

– Antoine de Saint-Exupéry

24
August

I have heard the mermaids singing,
each to each. I do not think
that they will sing to me.

– Thomas S. Eliot

25

August

You are only a prisoner
when you surrender.

– Tad Williams

26

August

Let us dance in the sun, wearing wild flowers in our hair.

– Susan Polis Schutz

27

August

The best time to make friends
is before you need them.

– Ethel Barrymore

28

August

The trouble with a kitten
is that eventually it becomes a cat.

– Ogden Nash

29

August

A friend is someone who knows
all about you and still loves you.

– Elbert Hubbard

30

August

There are two classes of travel: first class, and with children.

– Robert Charles Benchley

31

August

Our smile is younger than us.

– Roger Judrin

1

September

Fashion fades; only style remains the same.

– Coco Chanel

SEPTEMBER

2

September

An extravagance is something that
your spirit thinks is a necessity.

– Bernard Williams

3

September

And this that you call solitude
is in fact a big crowd.

– Dejan Stojanovic

4

September

The more people I make smile,
the more I smile.

– Richard Bandler

5

September

**If words were leaves,
would you prefer fall or spring?**

– Jarod Kintz

6

September

Autumn: the sun post scriptum.

– Pierre Véron

7

September

They once crossed a parrot and a tiger.
They don't know what it became,
but when it talks everyone listens.

– Andy Warhol

8

September

My car's very old.
My headlights have a cataract.

– *Milton Berle*

9

September

The cars we drive say a lot about us.

– *Alexandra Paul*

10
September

A door is what a dog
is perpetually on the wrong side of.

– Ogden Nash

11
September

My dog as a dog is a disaster,
but as a person is irreplaceable.

– Johannes Rau

12

September

A tourist is a fellow who drives thousands of miles
so he can be photographed standing in front of his car.

– Émile Genest

13

September

A driver reaches a destination by driving on that road,
not by laying back to enjoy the view.

– Nabil N. Jamal

14

September

Where the road bends abruptly,
take short steps.

– Ernest Bramah

15
September

I spend a lot of time upside down.
It increases the blood flow to the brain,
so it really helps your creativity.

– Daphne Guinness

16
September

There is nothing like staying
at home for real comfort.

– Jane Austen

17

September

Laugh and the world laughs with you,
snore and you sleep alone.

– Anthony Burgess

18

September

If people were meant to pop out of bed,
we'd all sleep in toasters.

– Jim Davis

19

September

People who keep dogs are cowards
who haven't got the guts to bite people themselves.

– *August Strindberg*

20

September

Do not make the mistake of treating your dogs like humans
or they will treat you like dogs.

– *Martha Scott*

21

September

A plumber is an adventurer
who traces leaky pipes
to their source.

– Arthur Baer

22

September

If someone derides you, laugh with him.

– Amadeus Voldben

23

September

There are moments when everything goes well;
don't be frightened, it won't last.

– Jules Renard

24

September

If you are going to drown your troubles in alcohol,
keep in mind that some problems can swim very well.

– Robert Musil

25

September

That's the funny thing about trying
to escape. You never really can.
Maybe temporarily, but not completely.

– Jennifer L. Armentrout

26

September

Life is what happens while
you are busy making other plans.

– John Lennon

27
September

Indecision may or may not be my problem.

– Jimmy Buffett

28
September

I've heard that hard work never killed anyone,
but I say why take the chance?

– Ronald Reagan

29

September

Idleness is fatal only to the mediocre.

– Albert Camus

30
September

Never play cat and mouse games
if you're a mouse.

– *Don Addis*

1

October

If you're going to be parents,
you must commit to being Muhammad Ali,
Albert Einstein and David Copperfield.

– Peter Schumacher

OCTOBER

2
October

I'm not shy I'm just holding back
my awesomeness so I won't intimidate.

– Anonymous

3
October

Sometimes the most dangerous place
can be the best hiding place
as no one will look for you there!

– Mehmet Murat Ildan

4

October

Happiness is a warm puppy.

– Charles M. Schulz

5

October

I have nothing against sharing the road with other drivers...
as long as they occupy the part of the road behind me.

– Anonymous

6

October

Any man who can drive safely while kissing a pretty girl
is simply not giving the kiss the attention it deserves.

– Albert Einstein

7

October

I've always thought that parallel parking
was my main talent.

– Calvin Trillin

8

October

Dogs need to sniff the ground:
it's their way of keeping up to date
on the latest news.

– Gustave Flaubert

9

October

The philosopher writes
about things you don't understand,
then makes you believe it's your fault.

– Boris Makaresko

10

October

Conscience is the inner voice
that warns us somebody may be looking.

– Henry L. Mencken

11

October

An elephant. A mouse built
to government specifications.

– Robert A. Heinlein

12

October

We call vices those entertainments
that we dare not try.

– Henry Miller

13
October

Very many drivers would have
beaten me if they had followed me.
They lost because they overtook me.

– Juan Manuel Fangio

14
October

I like talking to a brick wall:
it's the only thing in the world
that never contradicts me.

– Oscar Wilde

15

October

Animals are such agreeable friends,
they ask no questions; they pass no criticisms.

– George Eliot

16

October

If there's one thing I can't stand, it's the presumption
of those who think they are better than me.

– Freak Antoni

17

October

Never loan your car to anyone to whom you've given birth.

– Erma Bombeck

18

October

If everything seems to be under control,
then you're not going fast enough.

– Mario Andretti

19
October

Equipped with his five senses,
man explores the universe around him
and calls the adventure science.

– Edwin Hubble

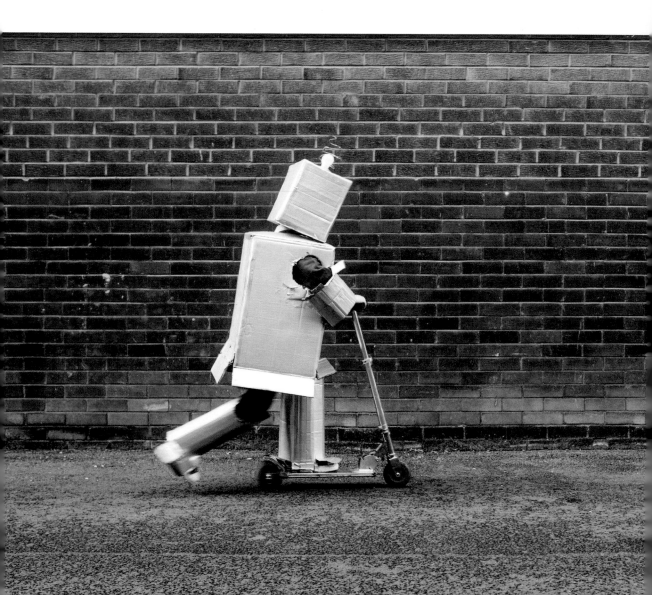

20
October

One way to get the most out of life
is to look upon it as an adventure.

– William Feather

21
October

If everyone followed the rules,
we wouldn't be human...
And I'd choose that than
being a Robot over any day.

– Jet Raymond Hodgkin

22
October

If it's reality you want, I suggest
you look out the window.

– Peter Stamm

23
October

It's more blessed to give than to receive.
Especially kittens.

– Bill Cosby

24
October

You can never own a cat.
The best you can do is be partners.

– Henry Swanson

25

October

When it comes to cars, only two varieties of people are possible: cowards and fools.

– *Russell Baker*

26
October

I am working hard,
I am carefully preparing my next error.

– Bertolt Brecht

27
October

It takes 72 muscles to frown,
and only 12 to smile.
You have to try once.

– Mordecai Richler

28

October

The secret of flight is this: you have to do it immediately,
before your body realizes it is defying the laws.

– Michael Cunningham

29

October

When you laugh you let yourself go, you are naked, you are exposed.
When someone laughs, you see his soul a little.

– Roberto Benigni

30
October

The first time I sang in the church choir,
two hundred people changed their religion.

– Fred Allen

31
October

Faith may be defined briefly
as an illogical belief in the
occurrence of the improbable.

– Henry L. Mencken

1

November

A house with old furniture
has no need of ghosts to be haunted.

– *Hope Mirrlees*

NOVEMBER

2
November

If you watch a scary movie together,
then the scariness is cut in half!

– Hidekaz Himaruya

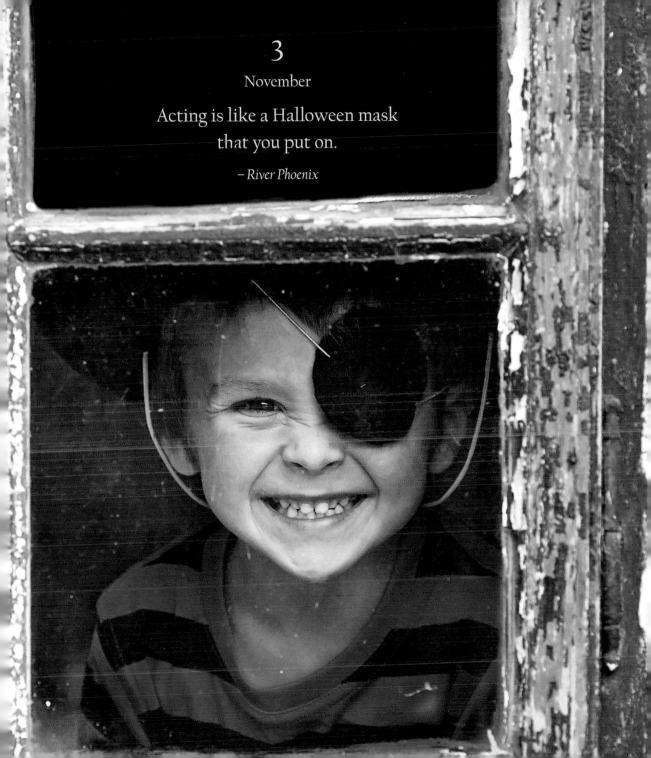

3

November

Acting is like a Halloween mask
that you put on.

– *River Phoenix*

4
November

You can only hold a smile for so long,
after that it's just teeth.

– Chuck Palahniuk

5
November

Have you ever noticed that anybody
driving slower than you is an idiot,
and anyone going faster than you
is a maniac.

– George Carlin

6

November

A secret's worth depends on the people
from whom it must be kept.

– *Carlos Ruiz Zafón*

7

November

The specialist knows more and more about less and less
and finally knows everything.

– *George Bernard Shaw*

8

November

We are all born mad.
Some remain so.

– Samuel Beckett

9

November

Yes, officer, I did see
the "speed limit" sign.
I just didn't see you.

– Anonymous

10

November

Fish deserve to be caught for
they are lazy. Two million years
of evolution and they still
haven't got out of the water.

– *Simon Munnery*

11

November

People say graffiti is ugly,
irresponsible and childish...
but that's only if it's done properly.

Banksy

12
November

I don't understand anything
about the ballet; all I know
is that during the intervals
the ballerinas stink
like horses.

– Anton Chekhov

13
November

He who finds a friend
with his own psychiatric disorder,
finds a treasure.

– Anonymous

14
November

He who wonders discovers
that this in itself is wonder.

– Maurits Escher

15
November

The cure for boredom is curiosity.
There is no cure for curiosity.

– Dorothy Parker

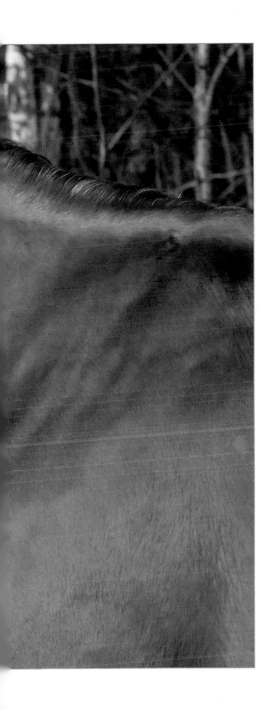

16
November

Life is like a mirror, it smiles at you
if you looks it smiling.

– Jim Morrison

17
November

Tell me what you boast of
and I'll tell you what you lack.

– Carlos Ruiz Zafón

18

November

He who mounts a wild elephant
goes where the wild elephant goes.

– Randolph Silliman Bourne

19

November

I hate television.
I hate it as much as peanuts.
But I can't stop eating peanuts.

– Orson Welles

20

November

Engineers like to solve problems.
If there are no problems handily available,
they will create their own problems.

– Scott Adams

21

November

There is no such thing as low maintenance or high maintenance,
just a bunch of women hoping for a capable mechanic.

– Liz Vassey

22

November

My fake plants died because
I did not pretend to water them.

– *Mitch Hedberg*

23

November

If money grew on the trees,
to me it would come given a Bonsai.

– *Boris Makaresko*

24

November

A well-trained dog will make no attempt to share your lunch.
He will just make you feel so guilty that you cannot enjoy it.

– Helen Thompson

25

November

If you think dogs can't count, try putting three dog biscuits
in your pocket and then giving Fido only two of them.

– Phil Pastoret

26

November

The first thing in life is to be able to seize the opportunity.
The second is to understand when to let it go.

– Benjamin Disraeli

27
November

My pillow is my best hair styler, every morning.
I wake up with a new hair style.

– Anonymous

28
November

It's hard to have a bad hair day when you're famous.

– Marion Jones

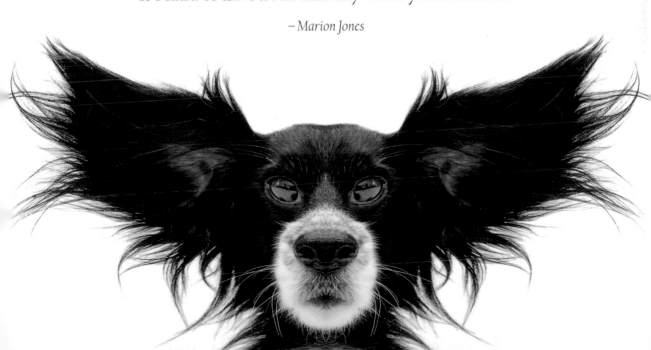

29

November

I believe that laughing is the best calorie burner.

– Audrey Hepburn

30
November

Donuts. Is there anything they can't do?

– Matt Groening

1

December

The wagon rests in winter,
the sleigh in summer, the horse never.

– Yiddish proverb

DECEMBER

2

December

The Eskimo has fifty names for snow
because it is important to them;
there ought to be as many for love.

– Margaret Atwood

3

December

No snowflake in an avalanche ever feels responsible.

– George Burns

4

December

The Universe is not only queerer than we suppose,
but queerer than we can suppose.

– John Burdon Sanderson Haldane

5

December

The best way to show your teeth
is with a smile.

– Henry Miller

6

December

The reason why machines
do more work than people
is that they never stop
to answer the telephone.

– Joey Adams

7

December

To err is human
but to really foul things up
you need a computer.

– Paul Ehrlich

8

December

I have lived with several Zen masters,
all of them cats.

– *Eckhart Tolle*

9

December

Cat's motto: no matter
what you've done wrong,
always try to make it
look like the dog.

– *Anonymous*

10

December

Cats have never completely got over
that in Ancient Egypt
they were worshipped as gods.

– *Pelham Grenville Wodehouse*

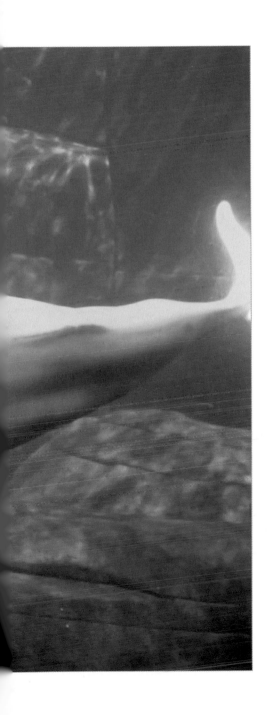

11
December

Each contact with a human being
is so rare, so precious,
one should preserve it.

– Anaïs Nin

12
December

Every man is an abyss,
and you get dizzy looking into it.

– Georg Buchner

13

December

Can any animal be
as disappointed as a dog
when you say "No"?

– *Jeffrey Moussaieff Masson*

14

December

If a dog's prayers were answered,
bones would rain from the sky.

– *Rainer Maria Rilke*

15
December

All animals are equal, but some animals
are more equal than others.

– George Orwell

16
December

Noise proves nothing. Often a hen who has merely laid
an egg cackles as if she laid an asteroid.

– Mark Twain

17
December

One small cat changes coming home
to an empty house to coming home.

- Pam Brown

18
December

A kitten is the delight of the household.
All day long a comedy is played out
by an incomparable actor.

– Champfleury

19
December

If it looks like a duck and sounds like a duck,
it could be a really ugly swan.

– *Timmothy Radman*

20
December

Everything in life is somewhere else, and you get there in a car.

– *Elwyn B. White*

21

December

The only creatures that are evolved enough
to convey pure love are dogs and infants.

– Johnny Depp

22

December

Babies are such a nice way to start people.

– Don Herold

23

December

A lot of people like snow.
I find it to be an unnecessary freezing of water.

– *Carl Reiner*

24

December

A snowball in the face is certainly the perfect beginning
to the end of a friendship.

– Leopold Fechtner

25
December

Christmas isn't a season.
It's a feeling.

Edna Ferber

26
December

Christmas makes me happy
no matter what time of year
it comes around.

– Bryan White

27

December

I recently took up ice sculpting.
Last night I made an ice cube.
This morning I made twelve,
I was prolific.

– Mitch Hedberg

28

December

It's worth melting
for a few people.

– Olaf (Frozen)

29
December

The dishes that my wife prepares for me melt in the mouth. I'd like her to learn to thaw them, first.

– Jack Klugman

30
December

In seed time learn,
in harvest teach,
in winter enjoy.

– William Blake

31

December

New year's resolution:
see last year's resolution:
see the year before's resolution:
see the year before's resolution ...

– Anonymous

LIST OF CONTRIBUTORS

PHOTO CREDITS

Project Editor
Valeria Manferto De Fabianis

Texts
Iceigeo, Milan

Graphic design
Maria Cucchi

Collaborating editor
Giorgio Ferrero

WHITE STAR PUBLISHERS

WS White Star Publishers® is a registered trademark
property of De Agostini Libri S.p.A.

© 2015 De Agostini Libri S.p.A.
Via G. da Verrazano, 15
28100 Novara, Italy
www.whitestar.it - www.deagostini.it

Translation: Iceigeo (Jonathan West)

ISBN 978-88-544-0949-1
1 2 3 4 5 6   19 18 17 16 15

Printed in China